Wayne Gretzky

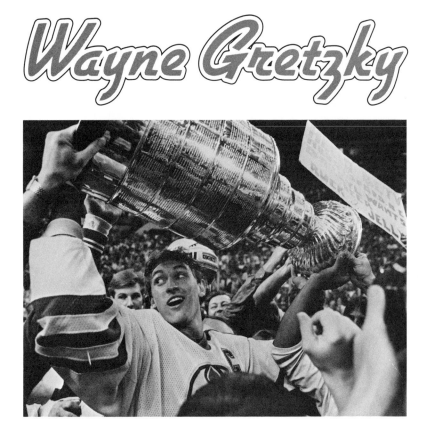

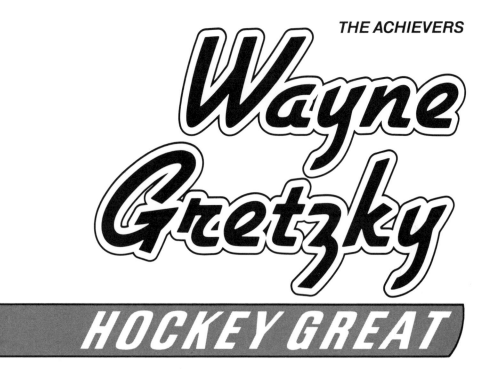

Wayne Gretzky

HOCKEY GREAT

Thomas R. Raber

Lerner Publications Company ■ Minneapolis

LIBRARY OF CONGRESS CATALOGING-IN-PUBLICATION DATA

Raber, Thomas R.
Wayne Gretzky, hockey great / Thomas R. Raber.
p. cm. — (The Achievers)
Summary: A biography of professional hockey star Wayne
Gretzky.
ISBN 0-8225-0539-8 (lib. bdg.)
1. Gretzky, Wayne, 1961-   —Juvenile literature.
2. Hockey players—Canada—Biography—Juvenile litera-
ture. [1. Gretzky, Wayne, 1961-   . 2. Hockey players]
I. Title. II. Series.
GV848.5.G73R33   1991
796.962'092—dc20
[B]   90-45834
[92]   CIP
                                            AC

Manufactured in the United States of America

1 2 3 4 5 6 7 8 9 10 00 99 98 97 96 95 94 93 92 91

Contents

The Great One

The Los Angeles Kings hockey team streaked down the ice toward the opposing goal. They were a blur of silver, black, and white uniforms. The Kings needed to score a goal. They trailed the Edmonton Oilers, 4-3, and only a minute remained in regulation time.

Skating with the Kings was number 99, center Wayne Gretzky. Wayne charged down the ice in his usual style. He skated with his helmet held low and his body bent at the waist. As always, he wore his hockey sweater tucked in at his right hip but flapping free on his left side.

Wayne was exhausted. Like many teams, the Oilers had assigned some of their toughest defensive players to cover him. They hoped to rough Wayne up and slow him down. The strategy had worked. In the second period, Wayne had been hit in the face with a hockey stick. He was not sure he would be able to play in the third period.

"I got my bell rung a couple of times," Wayne said later.

In addition, Wayne had played more than his share of time in the game. Most hockey players are assigned to a shift, or group, of teammates. They are rotated in and out of the game along with their shift. Wayne had been playing on more than one shift in this game.

But the game was on the line. The Kings, the visiting team in Edmonton, Canada, that day, needed Wayne on the ice—even if he did need a rest.

Wayne circled behind the Oilers' net. He set himself close to the left of the goal and waited. The puck came his way. It glanced off another player and skipped across the front of the net to Wayne's stick. With 53 seconds remaining, Wayne flipped the puck past the Oilers' goaltender and into the net.

Wayne turned and danced toward his teammates. The Kings left the bench to greet him. Wayne had tied the game.

But that's not all. Wayne Gretzky had become the all-time leading scorer in the history of professional hockey! This was the 641st goal of Wayne's career. When combined with his 1,210 assists, he had 1,851 career "points." The total put Wayne one point ahead of the record set by his boyhood idol, Gordie Howe of the Detroit Red Wings.

Wayne was given a three-minute standing ovation by the Edmonton fans. Wayne was a Los Angeles King now. But to the people of Canada, he was a hero.

For 10 seasons, Wayne had played in this building—the Northlands Coliseum in Edmonton, Alberta. The Edmonton Oilers had been hockey's Stanley Cup champions four times with Wayne as a member. And as an Oiler, Wayne had set more personal records than any player in hockey history.

The Edmonton fans had been the first to know Wayne as "the Great One." On this night—October 15, 1989—a sellout crowd of 17,503 Edmonton fans had come to the game.

A representative from the National Hockey League Hall of Fame collected the puck and stick Wayne used for the record. He picked up Wayne's jersey after the game. Wayne's wife, Janet, and his father, Walter, were on hand for the occasion, as was another man Wayne had asked to be there—Gordie Howe.

"I actually think Wayne felt a little bit bad about breaking the record," Howe said. "That's the kind of kid he is. He wanted to do it and he had to do it; he couldn't go the rest of the season without any points. But he didn't want to see me hurt by it all."

Howe was right. Wayne felt awkward about breaking his idol's record.

Gordie Howe had become hockey's leading scorer when he surpassed the Montreal Canadiens' great Maurice "Rocket" Richard on January 16, 1960. Howe took the lead with 965 points and added another 885 to his grand total before retiring in the 1970s. Howe's hold on the record had stood for almost 30 years—longer than Wayne Gretzky had been alive.

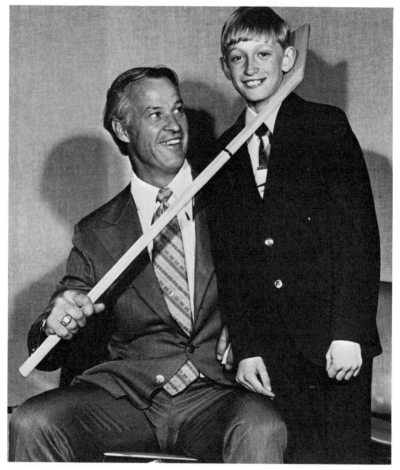

When Wayne was 11, he met his idol, Gordie Howe, for the first time. Even then, people thought Wayne might become a hockey legend just like Howe.

"It's one record I don't want to break," Wayne had said as he approached Howe's mark. "I think it's his record and he deserves it."

But early in Wayne's career, it was obvious that he was on a pace to pass Howe. As soon as he joined the NHL in 1979, Wayne began racking up points faster than any other player in the history of professional hockey. By the start of the 1989-90 season, Wayne was just 13 points behind Howe. The record-breaking point came in game number six. Wayne went on to score another goal that night to give the Kings a 5-4 victory over Edmonton.

Gordie Howe took 26 seasons and 1,767 games to compile his 801 goals and 1,049 assists. It took Wayne only 780 games and just over 10 seasons to collect 641 goals and 1,210 assists.

Critics say Howe played in a more difficult time against fiercer competition. They argue that Howe got most of his points when the National Hockey League included only six teams and was made up of the top talent in professional hockey. The NHL now has 21 teams and includes many less skilled players. But even if you cut Wayne's production rate in half, he still ranks as the best ever.

Wayne has accomplished more than any other player in the history of hockey. He has done it in less time, and he has done it with style. He holds or shares 50 NHL records. He has been an All-Star every year of his career. He has also been a Most Valuable Player nine times and the league's leading scorer eight times.

How did Wayne do it? How did he set so many hockey records so fast? Just what makes Wayne Gretzky "the Great One?"

The Soviet Union's finest hockey players were no match for the greatest in the world at this 1985 exhibition game.

Shooting for the Top

Wayne Gretzky skates untouched through a maze of defenders. He finds an open spot on the ice. The spot just *happens* to be where the puck slides next. Wayne settles the puck with his stick and sends a pass to a teammate who is skating at top speed. But Wayne is not watching his teammate take the pass. Wayne's eyes are focused on the spot he'll skate to next.

Sometimes Wayne's maneuvers fool the television cameras. Sometimes Wayne fools the fans, too. Most importantly, many of Wayne's moves fool some of hockey's finest players.

All of hockey's All-Stars have been graced with special gifts. Rocket Richard was a driving competitor and top shooter for the Montreal Canadiens during the 1940s and 1950s. Gordie Howe was a bruising checker and high scorer for the Detroit Red Wings during the 1950s and 1960s. Jean Beliveau was a

13

clutch playmaker for the Montreal Canadiens, and Bobby Hull was a feared scorer for the Chicago Blackhawks during the 1960s. In the 1970s, Bobby Orr was a stick-handling and skating whiz for the Boston Bruins.

Each was a record setter. Each was a superstar. But no one quite compares to Wayne Gretzky. Wayne was well known in Canada at age 11. By the time he was 19 years old, he was regarded as the best hockey player in the world. By age 25, he had broken almost every scoring record in hockey. Most hockey fans believe he is the greatest ever to play the game.

Wayne's hockey career began early. He was born on January 26, 1961, in Brantford, Ontario, a town of about 78,000 people located about 60 miles (96 kilometers) southwest of Toronto.

Wayne was the first child born to his parents, Walter and Phyllis Gretzky. Later, Wayne was joined by three brothers and a sister.

Wayne's parents encouraged him in sports from an early age. Even as a two-year-old, Wayne would scoot around the living room with a toy hockey stick and a ball. He would take shots against his grandmother, Mary. She would sit in a chair and serve as Wayne's goalie.

Wayne's father worked as a teletype repairman. As a young man, Walter Gretzky played Junior B— high-level amateur hockey in Canada. When Wayne was four, Walter built a small ice rink in the family's backyard. Mr. Gretzky even strung up a light so Wayne could use the rink at night. Wayne's father would water the rink every night with a lawn sprinkler. He would also shave hockey sticks down to Wayne's size.

As a boy, Wayne was small and shy. But when it came to hockey, he was larger than life.

"I was fortunate to have my dad as my first teacher," Wayne says. "He made the game simple and he made the game fun. He taught me the importance of a lot of hard work."

Wayne practiced hockey almost every day, either in his backyard or at nearby rinks. He and his father would do drills. Sometimes Wayne would skate patterns around cones and tin cans set on the ice. Other times Wayne would jump over sticks placed on the ice as he received passes from his father. In this way, the Gretzkys tried to imitate the obstacles Wayne would face in game situations. Often Wayne shot at targets his father had made. The targets got smaller as Wayne got better.

Sometimes Walter would throw a puck into a corner of the rink and urge Wayne to chase it. Wayne would follow the puck. His dad would yell, "Skate to where the puck's going to be, not to where it has been. Anticipate. Anticipate."

Wayne's knack for anticipating where the puck was going to bounce would prove to be one of his most outstanding talents.

Wayne practiced hard. Hockey was fun. No one needed to push him. "Wayne motivated himself," Walter says. But it's important to remember that much of Wayne's talent is an inborn gift.

When Wayne was six, he joined his first organized hockey team. The rest of his teammates were 10 years old. As Wayne grew, he continued to play with boys older than he was. He was almost always the youngest and smallest player on his teams, but he played as if he were much older. At age eight, he scored 104 goals in 40 games. At age nine, he had 196 goals and 316 points in 76 games. The next year, in 82 games, Wayne scored 378 goals.

Wayne's father went to all of Wayne's games. As they drove home, Wayne and his father would discuss situations that had come up during the game. They would review where Wayne or his teammates had been during a certain play and where, perhaps, they *should* have been.

By the time Wayne was 10, opposing teams began assigning specific players to check, or block, him. Wayne was quickly becoming a national celebrity in Canada. Hockey is the most popular sport in Canada, and news of the young superstar spread fast. The next year, Wayne played 9 games during a weekend tournament and scored 50 goals. Newspaper and television reporters wanted to interview Wayne. Some people wanted his autograph. It wasn't long before crowds at games became so large that Wayne sometimes needed a police escort just to get in and out of the arena.

When he was 11 years old, Wayne got a chance to meet his idol, Gordie Howe, at a sports banquet in Brantford.

Young Wayne Gretzky was unstoppable on the ice. Fans from all over Ontario came to Brantford to watch him play.

The pro star offered Wayne some advice the young player never forgot. "Make sure you keep practicing that backhand," Howe told Wayne. Wayne listened well. The backhand would become one of his best weapons.

The Gretzky children were all involved in sports as they were growing up. Wayne's sister, Kim, ran track. Keith Gretzky, the second of the four Gretzky boys, would go on to become a minor-league hockey player. Wayne played hockey, lacrosse, and baseball, and he also ran track.

By the time Wayne was a teenager, he had his sights set on a career in hockey. But two obstacles stood in Wayne's way. First, Wayne was not very big. At the time, pro teams were especially interested in big, strong players. Wayne was neither. Wayne's father advised him not to count on a pro career.

Second, Wayne was unhappy with his life. He should have been enjoying himself and his hockey talent. But he felt pressure, mainly from the parents of some of his teammates and opponents. They said Wayne was getting too much playing time. They said Wayne wanted all the glory for himself.

Wayne was sometimes jeered during games and hassled off the ice. People even called the Gretzkys' home to make rude comments. "The biggest disease in the world is jealousy," Wayne says. "If someone sees their child isn't doing as well as the next child, they take it out on the [successful] child. That's unfortunate."

One solution for Wayne was to leave home. He could live in another city. He could go to school and play hockey somewhere else. The idea sounded strange at first. Wayne's parents were against the move. But eventually the Gretzkys formed a plan.

Wayne moved to Toronto to live with family friends. He would go to school there and play Junior B hockey. Wayne was 14 years old. Some of the other Junior B players were 20!

"I wasn't enjoying the atmosphere in Brantford, the peer pressure," Wayne says. "It was so difficult for me just to go to school, such a big thing to knock off Gretzky.

"A lot of people thought I moved away from home to be a hockey player, but that's not why. I moved away to just try to escape all the pressures parents place on kids."

Wayne played Junior B hockey in Toronto for two years. Wayne called his family every night, and the Gretzkys drove to see as many of Wayne's games as they could.

At first, Wayne was excited about the move. But soon he felt lonely and sad.

"Lying in bed the first night in Toronto, I thought it was the greatest thing in the world," Wayne says. "Three days later it came to me, 'Oh, no, what am I doing here?' I was homesick for a year."

Wayne had to get used to living in a new place. He had to change schools a few times, and he had to do some schoolwork by mail. The experience was difficult, but it taught him independence.

Wayne was popular as a teenager. He could have had many dates. But he seldom asked anyone out, and he never saw anyone steadily. He didn't drink, smoke, or even drive. Wayne was into hockey.

"My father always told me to get what I wanted most and the rest would follow," Wayne says.

What Wayne wanted most was a hockey career.

By the time he was 17, Wayne began playing Junior A hockey for the Sault Sainte Marie Greyhounds. Until then, Wayne had always worn number 9 on his jersey in honor of his idol, Gordie Howe. But with Wayne's new team, the number was taken. So Wayne switched to 99—the number he has worn ever since.

Sault Sainte Marie, Ontario, is 500 miles (800 km) from Brantford. Again Wayne changed schools and moved in with family friends. His family was rarely able to travel to see his games. But by this time, it was clear that Wayne's hockey career would be taking him even farther away from home.

After a season of Junior A hockey, Wayne was voted the league rookie of the year and named its most sportsmanlike player. Then, just three years after leaving home, Wayne signed a lucrative professional contract with the Indianapolis Racers of the World Hockey Association (WHA). It was 1978. Wayne was just 17.

But the Racers, like many teams in the World Hockey Association, were having money problems.

Walter Gretzky (left) looks on as Wayne signs with the Edmonton Oilers on January 26, 1979—his 18th birthday.

Eight games into the 1978-79 season, Wayne and two other players were traded to the Edmonton Oilers of Alberta, Canada, for cash and future draft picks.

With the Oilers, Wayne became the WHA's rookie of the year. But the WHA folded the next season.

The Edmonton Oilers were one of four WHA teams absorbed into the National Hockey League for the 1979-80 season.

Wayne had realized his dream. He was a member of the National Hockey League. But it was only the beginning for the Great One.

Wayne skates off, leaving the puck squarely in the net behind a frustrated St. Louis Blues goalie.

The Right Angles

Wayne Gretzky burst into the National Hockey League. At 19, he was one of the youngest players in the league. Wayne was also small for the NHL at 6 feet (180 centimeters) and about 170 pounds (76.5 kilograms). But those obstacles were nothing new to Wayne. As usual, he dominated his competition.

In the 1979-80 season, his first in the NHL, Wayne won the Hart Trophy as the league's Most Valuable Player. He also won the Lady Byng Trophy as the league's most gentlemanly player. Wayne was the youngest player in history to win an NHL trophy. He was also the youngest ever to be named to the NHL All-Star team. Wayne compiled 137 points and finished third in the league scoring race.

But Wayne was just getting started. The next season, 1980-81, Wayne broke Bobby Orr's record for assists in a season. Orr had 102; Wayne had 109. At the same time, Wayne set a record for points in a season—

164—better than the previous all-time mark of 152 set by Phil Esposito when he skated for the Boston Bruins.

The next year Wayne recorded 212 points with 92 goals. He had broken Phil Esposito's record for most goals in a season by 16! In his first 39 games, Wayne scored 50 goals. That shattered Rocket Richard's mark of 50 goals in 50 games, which had stood since 1945 and had been equalled only once.

Wayne was just 21. But the marks he was setting were so far beyond the previous records that they were hard to put into perspective. Wayne was rewriting the hockey record books and changing the face of the game.

"Hockey needed a shot in the arm when he came along," explains Hall of Famer Bobby Hull. "It needed a champion. People are again relating to hockey as a game of skill, because that's the way Wayne plays."

Some fans thought of hockey as merely a bruising game—until Wayne Gretzky came along. Wayne is an example of the finesse of the game. He is not a rough-and-tough hockey player. He isn't big, and a rough style wouldn't suit him anyway. Instead, Wayne's game is marked by quickness, agility, and spirit.

Wayne is not an especially graceful skater, and his skating speed is about average. But he has excellent balance, an extremely accurate shot, and uncanny puck-handling skills.

When the Great Gretzky joined the NHL, hockey records began to crumble. Wayne quickly surpassed the marks for points and goals set by Phil Esposito (above) and the record for assists held by Bobby Orr (left).

It's not size or speed that allows Wayne to dominate the game of hockey, it's his intense concentration.

What many experts talk about is Wayne's "hockey sense." He seems to anticipate where the puck is headed next. He is able to look two or three plays ahead in the game and then choose the best course of action. Some experts believe that Wayne sees the game action at a slower speed than the average player. This gift gives him more time to analyze situations and carry out his moves.

Most pro players look at the individual men on the ice, but Wayne looks at situations. He sees all of his teammates as part of the play—not just the one or two players who are in his sight. He thinks about the entire rink—not just the ice that is in front of him.

Wayne's vision is valuable even when he does not have the puck. He knows how to play without the puck and how to get open. He not only sees openings, he creates them. Wayne calls hockey a game of geometry—a game of angles that is constantly changing.

"People talk about skating, puck handling, and shooting," Wayne says, "but the whole sport is angles and caroms [rebounds], forgetting the straight direction the puck is going, calculating where it will be diverted, factoring in all the interruptions. Basically my whole game is angles."

Much of Wayne's ability comes naturally. No amount of practice could turn a lesser athlete into Wayne Gretzky. But Wayne has practiced tirelessly to make the most of his gifts.

"I'm the first to admit I've been God blessed," Wayne says, "but I also know I've worked hard for everything I got."

Like most champions, Wayne has the ability to rise to an occasion. He is at his best when the pressure is greatest. Wayne also has a knack for making his teammates play better, too. He sets them up with his good passes. But he also inspires them to play their best.

"You see him working so hard every *second*. This is the best player in the world, so how can you not *try* to work that hard?" says Kings' left wing Luc Robitaille.

Wayne plays in the thick of the action, but he uses his balance and anticipation to avoid collisions. Opponents may connect with a piece of Wayne, but he is often able to lean away from the blow and soften the impact.

"There isn't a center in the league I can outmuscle," Wayne admits. "I played a lot of lacrosse, and that taught me how to roll with checks, slip away from them. I only get hit head-on two or three times a year. People say players in the NHL won't hit me. They all want to hit me. But they have to catch me first!"

Wayne has weaknesses too. Some say Wayne is not a good player on defense. But just Wayne's presence on the ice is a type of defense. When Wayne is playing, the opposition must think about stopping him. "If I've got it [the puck], they can't score," Wayne says. And even when Wayne doesn't have the puck, opponents have to keep an eye on him, sometimes leaving Wayne's teammates open in the process.

Rocket Richard's record of 50 goals in 50 games stood for 36 years until Wayne shattered it in a mere 39 games.

Hockey's greatest talents are quick to praise Wayne's skill. "He passes far better than anybody I've ever seen and he thinks so far ahead," says Bobby Orr.

"Wayne is a perfectionist who is blessed with the gift of total concentration," says Gordie Howe.

"I've seen some good skaters, but they were never like Gretzky," says Rocket Richard. "There's no way anyone will stop him from being the greatest star in hockey."

Great Seasons

By 1982, nothing Wayne accomplished came as a complete surprise. In fact, many of the records Wayne was breaking were his own. Wayne scored more than 200 points in four out of five seasons between 1981 and 1986. In 1985-86, he had 163 assists and 215 total points—marks that still stand as Wayne's best and all of hockey's best for a season. The 200-point plateau was once unimaginable in hockey. For Wayne, however, it became almost a yearly occurrence.

Wayne enjoyed his records. But he was most enthusiastic about winning. In the 1982-83 season, the Oilers were swept out of the Stanley Cup playoffs in four games by the New York Islanders. The Islanders held Wayne without a goal and went on to win their fourth consecutive Stanley Cup.

But the next year, 1983-84, provided one of Wayne's best rewards. Edmonton won its first Stanley Cup in Wayne's first year as captain of the team. Wayne also was the NHL's Most Valuable Player for the fifth time, and he compiled 205 points.

Wayne had an amazing scoring streak that season. He scored at least one point in 51 straight games. It was a sports feat often compared to baseball Hall of Famer Joe DiMaggio hitting safely in 56 straight games for the New York Yankees in 1941. It's a record likely to stand for a long, long time.

Even Wayne was impressed by what he had done.

"This may have been one of the harder records to break," Wayne said afterwards. "When you score 90 goals or break the record for points, you can do that over 80 games. But the streak itself is pressure every night to be at your best, be consistent game in and game out."

Wayne's best feeling, however, came from being a winner. With their Stanley Cup championship, Wayne and the Oilers stood in the way of hockey history. A victory would have given the New York Islanders a record-tying five consecutive Stanley Cups.

"I enjoy hockey even more now that I can say I'm a champion," Wayne said then. "To be champion changes everything, just the way you feel about coming to the rink. Many a time I've stared and stared at the Stanley Cup."

Jubilant Oilers, including Mark Messier, Wayne, and Kevin Lowe, show off their fourth Stanley Cup trophy.

The Edmonton Oilers went on to win four Stanley Cups with Wayne. The Oilers became not only one of the most successful teams but also one of the most exciting. Wayne was surrounded by other star players such as Jari Kurri, Mark Messier, Kevin Lowe, and Paul Coffey. And Wayne continued to improve.

In 1984-85, the Oilers won their second straight Stanley Cup. Wayne bettered his record for assists with 135. Some observers noticed a good change in Wayne. He was becoming more mature on the ice. Wayne used to be called a "wimp," a "whiner," or a "crybaby" by some critics.

Wayne used to have a reputation for whining to officials. He would sometimes take "dives" on the ice. If an opponent collided with him, Wayne might exaggerate his fall. He might lie on the ice just a bit too long before getting up. Wayne was hoping the game official would call a penalty against the opposing player.

But no more. Wayne had changed his ways. He didn't like his reputation as a complainer. "The big thing with me is that I play emotionally," Wayne says. "I used to let the emotion run away with me. If I got fouled, I'd blame the ref or the other player. Now my attitude is, if the ref calls it, fine; if not, I'm not going to change his mind."

In 1985-86, Wayne enjoyed his finest scoring season. But the Oilers were eliminated by the Calgary Flames in the quarterfinals of the Stanley Cup play-offs. In the deciding game, Steve Smith, a rookie defenseman, accidentally knocked the puck into his own net. The Flames won the game by a single goal. Smith's error had cost the defending champion Oilers a chance to make it three straight post-season championships.

But a year later, in the 1986-87 season, the Oilers beat the Philadelphia Flyers in seven games for the cup. Wayne led the league in scoring during the regular season and in the play-offs. After the Oilers' championship victory, Wayne showed why he was the team captain.

Even when the big bruisers knock Wayne off his feet, he keeps his cool.

Wayne accepted the Stanley Cup trophy at center ice and searched for Steve Smith. He wanted Smith to be the first Oiler teammate to hold the cup high.

A whole year had gone by. But Wayne had not forgotten how bad Steve Smith must have felt about his mistake.

The year 1987 was important in other ways for Wayne. In February, Wayne led a team of NHL All-Stars in a two-game series against the national team of the Soviet Union. The two teams each won a game in the series, which was played in Quebec, Canada. Wayne was voted the NHL team's Most Valuable Player.

That September, Wayne served as captain of Team Canada, a hockey team that represented Canada against five other countries in the Canada Cup tournament. Wayne led all tournament players in points with 3 goals and 18 assists in 9 games. Team Canada won the event by defeating the Soviet Union. Many spectators rated Canada's three play-off games against the Soviets to be some of the most exciting hockey ever played. The score of all three games was 6-5, and the first two games were decided in overtime.

Wayne's playmaking was decisive in the final game. With less than a minute and a half left in the game, Wayne sent a perfect pass to teammate Mario Lemieux (who plays in the NHL for the Pittsburgh Penguins). Lemieux took Wayne's pass and shot home the winning goal.

"The Canada Cup was my greatest thrill," Wayne said then. "I said to the boys in the dressing room, 'Every kid in Canada would love to be playing right now and doing what we're doing,' and it's true."

Wayne returned to his NHL duties for the 1987-88 season. Yet Wayne was under stress. The pressure of being the most famous person in Canada seemed to be wearing him down. Since he was a young boy, Wayne had been in the national spotlight. For years he had handled the attention pretty well. But now Wayne was tired.

"I guess it finally caught up with me," Wayne said.

Wayne began to talk of retiring. He was only 26, but he had been playing hockey a long time. Some fans whispered that Wayne was slowing down.

In the 1987-88 season, Wayne "lost" the Hart Trophy for the Most Valuable Player to Mario Lemieux. Wayne had owned the award for eight straight seasons. Wayne also "lost" the scoring title he'd had for seven years. There too, Lemieux was the winner.

Wayne's yearly totals would have been great for any other player. But his 40 goals were a career low. His 149 points marked his lowest output since he recorded 137 as a rookie.

On December 30, 1987, Wayne was knocked into a goal post. He sprained ligaments in his left knee. The injury kept him out of 13 games. Later in the season, an errant stick caught him in the eye and sidelined him for three games.

During Wayne's first absence, Lemieux, the big center from Pittsburgh, took over the scoring lead. Gretzky never could catch him.

At the Canada Cup tournament, Wayne and Guy Lafleur (left) showed that Canada has the best hockey players in the world.

Was the Great Gretzky slowing down? Wayne quickly answered the question. He led the league in assists for the ninth straight season and led the Oilers to yet another Stanley Cup championship. He set an NHL record for most assists in the play-offs, 31 in 19 games, and most in the series final, with 10. He earned his second Conn Smythe Trophy as the best player in the play-offs.

Wayne's teammate Mark Messier said it simply, "He played like he never has before."

Traded

After winning the Stanley Cup in 1988, Wayne had even more reason to celebrate. On the afternoon of July 16, 1988, he married American movie actress Janet Jones in Edmonton.

It was a day of national celebration in Canada. There were 600 guests at the wedding, and a large crowd of well-wishers gathered for blocks around the church.

The wedding party included Wayne's Edmonton teammates Kevin Lowe, Mark Messier, and Paul Coffey, Wayne's three younger brothers, Brent, Keith, and Glen, and Wayne's sister, Kim.

"It was a tough wedding because we had to try to satisfy not only friends and family, we had to satisfy fans, try to satisfy the media. It was hard," Wayne says. "We were working almost full time on the wedding. My wife was pregnant. It was an emotional time."

Fans and photographers flocked to Edmonton to see Wayne marry Janet Jones.

Wayne had met Janet on the set of an American television show called "Dance Fever." Janet was a regular dancer on the show, and Wayne appeared one time as a celebrity judge.

Wayne and Janet share a love of sports. Janet not only dances, she is a swimmer and diver who also enjoys softball. As an actress, she knows the demands of performing in public.

"She's a great lady who understands the pressures that I'm under," Wayne said. "Obviously, being in pressure situations herself, she can relate to it."

Wayne and Janet announced their engagement in January 1988. Canada had six months to anticipate the event. It was probably the most publicized wedding in Canadian history.

Less than a month after the wedding, on August 9, 1988, Wayne Gretzky again found himself in the news. There was nothing unusual about that. But the headlines this time were almost unthinkable to hockey fans. The great Wayne Gretzky had been *traded*. The Oilers had sent Wayne and two other players to the Los Angeles Kings. In return, the Kings sent the Oilers two players, three future first-round draft choices, and $15 million.

At a press conference in Edmonton, Wayne was in tears. He choked out a good-bye to the people of Edmonton. Then he was off on a plane heading to Los Angeles.

Hockey fans weren't the only people shocked. Wayne was a national Canadian hero. Just 24 days earlier, the whole country had gone crazy over his wedding. But now Canadians felt they had lost Wayne to the United States!

On the day Wayne was traded, a man from a swimming pool company came to the home of Wayne's parents. The man was there to see about building a pool in the Gretzkys' backyard—on the spot where Wayne's father had built the ice rink. Wayne knew about the pool. In fact, it was a gift from Wayne and Janet. But a piece of hockey history was about to be buried with the project. Mr. Gretzky said, "He's been after me for a couple of years to put it in. Now I guess we might as well."

Some Oiler fans made up rude signs and sayings about the man who traded Wayne, Oilers' owner Peter Pocklington. Oiler defenseman Kevin Lowe said what was on many fans' minds: "How do you replace Wayne Gretzky?"

Wayne was as stunned as anyone.

"At that point, I felt like everyone else. I couldn't believe it was happening. It wasn't as if we had just lost. We had just won the Stanley Cup for the fourth time in five years. I'd had, arguably, my best play-off ever. I won the Conn Smythe, and all of a sudden, I'm traded."

The news of the trade was surrounded by rumors.

Canadians were upset that their greatest hero would be lost to the United States.

Some said Wayne had a hunch he would be traded. His contract was to expire in 1992, and he would be free to play for another team. The Oilers would lose their star player and get nothing in return. Many people expected the Oilers to trade Wayne before the contract expired.

If a trade was sure to come, rumors said, Wayne wanted to go to a team he liked. Some said Wayne *asked* the Oilers to trade him. Peter Pocklington, hoping to avoid a trade altogether, offered to give Wayne a new contract.

The trade to Los Angeles was surrounded by controversy. Here, Kings owner Bruce McNall (left), Wayne, and Oilers owner Peter Pocklington (right) speak to the press.

But Wayne did not want to give up the chance to become a free agent and see what other teams would offer to pay him. Some people thought Wayne was greedy not to agree to sign up with the Oilers again. Others thought he was smart to find out what he was worth to other teams.

Some people blamed the trade on Wayne's wife. Janet Gretzky is an actress. Some thought she wanted Wayne traded to Los Angeles so she could be closer to her career in Hollywood. The rumor irritated Wayne. He said his wife was not behind the trade.

Wayne was also angry at Peter Pocklington. The Oilers' owner said Wayne faked his tears at the press conference announcing the trade. Wayne was hurt by what Pocklington had said, and Wayne's disappointment made it easier to leave the Oilers' team.

It didn't take long for Wayne to see the good side of being traded. Going to Los Angeles would allow him and his new family to live a more normal life. Southern California is filled with famous people. There, Wayne would blend in. He wouldn't stand alone as one big star.

Wayne's move to Los Angeles would be like his move away from home at 14. It would give him a chance to be *less* famous. "I'm only in the sports section here," Wayne said of Los Angeles.

Wayne was also concerned for his family's privacy. His first baby was due in January 1989. "People won't know who our kids are. That wouldn't have been possible in Canada.

"Let's face it. The child would be under a microscope living in Canada. In L.A., he's just another child in the crowd.

"Everybody always treated us first-class there [in Edmonton]," Wayne says. "But we had absolutely no privacy. . . . You always felt like you were on display."

In Los Angeles, Wayne quickly felt at home. Wayne looked strange at first, not wearing the Oilers' colors. But in the season opener against the Detroit Red Wings, Wayne scored on the first shot he took. He added three assists in the game and helped the Kings win, 8-2. Wayne showed he was the same player he'd always been.

The Kings drew a sellout crowd for the home opener of 1988. The team got off to a 4-0 start, the best in its history. Average attendance at Kings' games increased by more than 3,200 people per game. Many were new fans, coming to watch Wayne.

Before Wayne joined the Kings, they had rarely been a successful team. But with Wayne, they posted the fourth best record in the league: 42-31-7 in the regular season. They finished second in the Smythe Division, ahead of the Oilers. The Kings eliminated the now "Wayneless" defending champion Oilers in the first round of the play-offs. The Kings were later eliminated in the division finals.

The next year, Wayne became the highest-scoring hockey player of all time. It was Wayne's second season with the Kings, and he felt confident. "This year, especially, I am not the new kid on the block anymore and feel a lot more comfortable about everything," Wayne said.

The Kings had never been a great hockey club. But when Wayne moved to Los Angeles, the team's prospects changed dramatically.

Wayne was back up to speed. Once again, he led the league in scoring. But the Kings were still a mediocre team; they placed fourth in the Smythe Division. Their finish showed that Wayne couldn't do it alone. Many fans noticed that Wayne wasn't surrounded by as many talented players as he had been with the Oilers.

In the 1990 division semifinals, the Kings beat Calgary in six games. But Edmonton then swept the Kings 4-0 in the division finals.

Wayne was hurt by a hard check late in the season. He missed the last five regular-season games and three play-off games because of a sore back.

"As ecstatic as we were last year after beating Edmonton [in the division semifinals], I'm disappointed," Wayne said at the season's end. "I hate losing."

More in Store

A rookie defenseman felt nervous. It was his first NHL practice session. In his first drill, he was assigned to stop his teammate Wayne Gretzky on a rush down the ice.

Wayne charged toward the rookie along with two other teammates. The rookie and a partner needed to stop the 3-on-2 break. The rookie's chances weren't good against Wayne Gretzky. But wow! The rookie broke up the rush!

Actually, Wayne let the rookie stop the play. He knew the rookie would be nervous. And Wayne's "assist" helped calm the new man down.

Wayne loves to show off his hockey skills, but he doesn't always want to be the star of the show. In fact, Wayne has always been shy. He is not fully at ease with the attention he draws. He is soft-spoken, and he usually tries to direct attention away from himself. He always tries to avoid controversy.

Wayne and brother Brent

"I don't think anybody needs to get into a war of words," Wayne says. "I never argue with people. You can't win. I just walk away from it. If I order a steak medium rare and it comes back well done, I eat it. Life's too short. I've got more important things in life to worry about."

The most important thing in Wayne's life is his family. Wayne and Janet have two children. Their daughter, Paulina, was born in December 1988, and a son, Ty Robert, was born in July 1990. The Gretzkys plan to have more children. They have plenty of room in their big house in Encino, California, near Los Angeles. Wayne also remains very close to his family back in Brantford.

"Hockey will always be number two to my family," Wayne says. "And to me, friends are more important than business."

Some of Wayne's best friends are hockey players, both from the Oilers and the Kings. He is especially close to his ex-Edmonton teammates, Kevin Lowe, Mark Messier, and Paul Coffey.

Wayne has made a lot of money playing hockey. He makes about $3 million a year, including his earnings from commercial endorsements. But despite his wealth, Wayne says, "I'd rather be broke and have friends than be rich and not have friends. That's my philosophy, because with friends you can go a long way. With money, you can become awfully lonely."

Wayne has a good reputation for signing autographs and meeting fans. Wayne could keep to himself and avoid the public. Even though he is still shy, Wayne likes to meet people. He has become an ambassador for the sport of hockey. He handles the demands of fame well because he enjoys it.

"A lot of athletes forget who they are and how they got where they are," Wayne says. "My main focus is hockey, but I believe you have to give something back to the game.

"I owe everything I have to hockey. It's given me . . . a chance to see the world, to meet some great people. I get paid a lot of money for something that I love to do. And when you think you're bigger than your sport, you're in trouble."

Wayne is idolized by young sports fans.

Wayne is respected by all of the sports world, not just followers of hockey. Wayne was selected as the best athlete of the 1980s in a poll conducted by the Associated Press. He finished far ahead of such top athletes as football player Joe Montana, basketball player Earvin "Magic" Johnson, and track-and-field star Carl Lewis.

Wayne's respect in the sports world is significant. While hockey is foremost in Canada, it is not as popular in the United States. In many parts of the U.S., hockey is not aired regularly on television. But if some American people know nothing else about hockey, they know about Wayne Gretzky.

Wayne is proud of his achievements and wants to stay recognized for his talent. But Wayne is sympathetic to Mario Lemieux and the other players who are compared to him. He knows it's just a matter of time before younger players begin to chip away at his records the way he gunned for the marks set by Gordie Howe, Phil Esposito, and Montreal Canadien Guy Lafleur.

Wayne welcomes the new stars into the league for the good of hockey. More star players means more fan interest. Wayne knows that's good for the game.

In the 1988-89 season, Wayne had 168 points, which was the eighth highest total in the history of the NHL. Yet Lemieux, not Wayne, won the Art Ross scoring trophy for the second straight year. In the

1989-90 season, his second with the Kings, Wayne's legs lacked spring, and he admitted to being tired. Still he scored 40 goals and led the league in assists. He took back the scoring lead from Mario Lemieux by leading the league with 142 points.

Younger players such as Mario Lemieux threaten to knock Gretzky off his pedestal.

Gretzky is still great. But Wayne has learned to conserve his energy now. He continues to avoid collisions in the "heavy traffic" on the ice. He also saves energy for many off-the-ice projects.

Wayne spends much of his time working for charity. He is active in an annual softball tournament in Brantford that benefits the Canadian National Institute for the Blind. Wayne started the tourney years ago, after being inspired by the cheery attitude of a blind wrestler he met from northern Ontario.

Wayne plays golf. He likes to fish. And when he wants to relax, Wayne loves to watch television — especially professional sports and soap operas. Once he even acted in a soap opera, and he has been a guest on TV talk shows many times.

Wayne enjoys owning flashy automobiles. But he is uneasy about another type of transportation: airplanes. He even underwent hypnosis in 1982 to help him overcome his fear. At one time Wayne thought his nervousness about flying might shorten his career.

"I'm very uncomfortable on an airplane so I can't sleep," Wayne says. This can be a serious problem for someone whose professional schedule keeps him flying from city to city all year round.

Wayne says it helps if he doesn't sit down on the plane. When possible, he paces the plane, talks to other people, and tries to fool himself into believing he's on the ground. Sometimes on Canadian airlines, where government regulations allow it, Wayne walks into the cockpit to talk to the pilots. The pilots are glad to see him, and Wayne feels comfortable there. "The pilots can reassure me," Wayne says.

Hockey has taken up most of Wayne's life. But Wayne is well aware there is more to the world than hockey sticks and pucks. "Lots of times I wished I'd gone to university," Wayne says. "But I've lived a great life, been to lots of places, and I owe it all to hockey. You can't have it all."

Wayne no longer talks about a premature retirement. "When I said I was going to retire at 30, I was absolutely serious," Wayne says. "But now it is enjoyable to go to the rink . . . it is all a breath of fresh air."

And Wayne still has records to set. He could catch Gordie Howe's all-time record for goals scored. Wayne scored his 2,000th point in October 1990, and some fans think he could score another 1,000 before he's through. But Wayne is uncomfortable comparing himself to other hockey stars. He would never call himself "the greatest."

"In my mind Gordie Howe is the best player who ever played hockey and the best man who ever played sports." Wayne says. "I just want to be remembered as a guy who always worked hard . . . when I've had an off night I've always forced myself to bounce back."

Wayne is modest, but he knows the significance of his accomplishments. He knows his achievements have inspired young players. "The first time I stood on the ice beside [NHL All-Star] Marcel Dionne, I was 18," Wayne says. "I can remember exactly how excited I was. I've seen that same look in younger eyes."

Gretzky and Howe show off the pucks that they hit to set their historic scoring records. The pucks are kept in the NHL Hall of Fame.

After a decade of professional hockey, Wayne still hits the ice with a smile. Even in pressure games, hockey is still fun. The rink is the place where Wayne can most be himself—where he can be happiest.

WAYNE GRETZKY
Professional hockey statistics

Regular Season

YEAR	TEAM	LEAGUE	GAMES	GOALS	ASSISTS	POINTS	PENALTY MINUTES
1978-79	Indianapolis Racers	WHA	8	3	3	6	0
1978-79	Edmonton Oilers	WHA	72	43	61	104	19
1979-80	Edmonton Oilers	NHL	79	51	86	137	21
1980-81	Edmonton Oilers	NHL	80	55	109	164	28
1981-82	Edmonton Oilers	NHL	80	92	120	212	26
1982-83	Edmonton Oilers	NHL	80	71	125	196	59
1983-84	Edmonton Oilers	NHL	74	87	118	205	39
1984-85	Edmonton Oilers	NHL	80	73	135	208	52
1985-86	Edmonton Oilers	NHL	80	52	163	215	46
1986-87	Edmonton Oilers	NHL	79	62	121	183	28
1987-88	Edmonton Oilers	NHL	64	40	109	149	24
1988-89	Los Angeles Kings	NHL	78	54	114	168	26
1989-90	Los Angeles Kings	NHL	73	40	102	142	42

Play-offs

YEAR	GAMES	GOALS	ASSISTS	POINTS	PENALTY MINUTES
1978-79	13	10	10	20	2
1979-80	3	2	1	3	0
1980-81	9	7	14	21	4
1981-82	5	5	7	12	8
1982-83	16	12	26	38	4
1983-84	19	13	22	35	12
1984-85	18	17	30	47	4
1985-86	10	8	11	19	2
1986-87	21	5	29	34	6
1987-88	19	12	31	43	16
1988-89	11	5	17	22	0
1989-90	7	3	7	10	0

ACKNOWLEDGMENTS

Photographs are reproduced through the courtesy of: Westfile/Bill McKeown, pp. 1, 2, 6, 35, 46, 60; Brantford Expositor, pp. 10, 15, 18, 54; Westfile/Bob Mummery, pp. 12, 37, 42; Westfile Archive, pp. 22, 40, 59, 63; Bill McKeown, pp. 24, 28; Al Ruelle, p. 27 (both); Montreal Canadiens, p. 31; Bob Mummery, pp. 45, 64; Doug Maclellan, pp. 49, 52; Pittsburgh Penguins, p. 56.

Front cover photograph: Photography Ink. Back cover photograph: Doug Maclellan.

64